UNLOCK YOUR BIBLE:

The Key to Understanding and Applying the Scriptures in Your Life

Dr. Steve McVey
Author of **Grace Walk**

Cover design by Jennifer Shaw

UNLOCK YOUR BIBLE:
The Key To Understanding And Applying Scriptures In Your Life

Copyright © 2013 by Steve McVey
Published by Grace Walk Resources, LLC
Atlanta, Georgia
www.gracewalkresources.com

ISBN-13: 978-1492885115

ISBN-10: 1492885118

TABLE OF CONTENTS

✦ ✦

✦✦

What Others Say

In *Unlock Your Bible,* my friend Steve McVey addresses one of the most critical needs within Christendom today. Remember the old saying– "How do I know? The Bible tells me so"? But today, competing voices from all across the denominational spectrum attribute widely differing meanings and interpretations about specific biblical passages. So, how do we know? ...

This book addresses that pressing issue and more– and does so in a short, easy to read eBook! Steve will help you to answer questions such as: *From what perspective should I read the Bible? What is the real significance of the New Covenant--and when did it begin? What* (Hint: though it might appear to give the answer away, perhaps it's better to ask *"Who"*) *is the goal of Bible Study?*

✦ ✦

Unlock Your Bible is a much-needed, concise course in understanding the Bible. Don't miss this helpful instruction from one of today's leading voices about God's amazing grace.

— Greg Albrecht, President
Plain Truth Ministries

*****

Dr. Steve McVey is an inspiring teacher with an authentic revelation of the grace of God. While Steve possesses a profound theological grasp of the scriptures, I am always impressed with his relatable approach. The mark of an effective teacher is to seamlessly blend depth with simplicity. That is exactly what Steve does here.

The Gospel is simple enough for a child to understand, and yet so deep, it is the glory of kings to search it out. Jesus Christ is the Word of God. He is the Ultimate Text by which we should see all of the scriptures. Steve unpacks this very truth, giving you a proper lens for approaching the Bible from a New

✦✦

Covenant perspective. It threatens to liberate you and kindle a ravenous hunger for the Word.

Steve has richly blessed my life, and I know this book will bless yours. Step back and begin to see Jesus and His finished work dripping from every page.

> – John Crowder,
> *Sons of Thunder Ministries & Publications*

*****

Once again Steve McVey does an outstanding job in breaking down a difficult topic and making it very practical and easy to understand. *Unlock Your Bible* is an excellent read whether you are an experienced Bible student or new to the grace walk. We discover early in the book the "master key" to understanding the Bible, and then in each chapter we learn to use the master key to rightly divide and unlock the truth of God's Word.

✦ ✦

This book is not only a great tool for personal growth, but also a wonderful resource for home groups, Sunday school or discipleship classes. I encourage you to take a little time and learn how to *Unlock Your Bible*.

— Don Keathley, Founder/Senior Pastor
Grace Point Community Church
Houston, Texas

*****

In His book *Unlock Your Bible,* Dr Steve McVey brilliantly and succinctly explains how to clearly understand the framework of Scripture, in a way that brings empowering yet practical simplicity to potentially complex thoughts. He demonstrates his capacity to take what have been historically viewed as "academic principles" and deliver them in a down to earth manner that enables all readers to learn the joy of experientially knowing God, as He intends to be known.

To bring the right context to what we read in Scripture is essential to understanding and experiencing the nature of our loving Father. To be able to understand

✦✦

the difference between covenants, the centrality of Jesus in Scripture, and the importance of determining the audience of Scripture are hugely beneficial. Steve explains how this all fits together extremely well.

I highly recommend this book to you.

— Phil Linden, Senior Pastor
Vantage Point Church
Melbourne, Australia

*****

"If you're going to read a Bible, or if you simply want to talk about the Bible, you've got to have what Steve McVey's book, *Unlock Your Bible* gives. In a concise and beautifully written manner, Steve offers the reader the most immediately practical and overwhelmingly helpful distinctions concerning one's understanding of the Bible that I have ever found.

Frankly, your view of God, yourself and everyone else, hinges upon your understanding of these simple keys. While reading this book, you'll think, "Oh! I totally get it! I love this!"

✦ ✦

So, if you'd like to see why God thinks the gospel is such good news, this will give you the foundation that provides the view.

> – Ralph Harris, author of *God's Astounding Opinion of You*
> President, *LifeCourse Ministries*

*****

Unlock your Bible could just as easily have been named *Unlocking Your Heart*. Steve McVey doesn't introduce us to a new academic discipline in this book. He creates a new hunger to see the love of God and the Grace of Christ in every book of the Bible. I believe that *Unlock your Bible* should be a First Step reading for everyone who wants to experience the Wonder of God's Love.

> – Roger Dean, CEO
> *Atlanta Computer Sales*

✦ ✦

Introduction

"I gave up on reading the Bible a long time ago," Sean told me one day after he had heard me speak at a conference.

"Really?" I asked. "Any particular reason why?"

"Because it seems like outdated writings that nobody today would find relevant to their lives, if they are honest," Sean replied. "I mean, think about it. Even Jesus Himself said some very strange things. To tell people to love their enemies isn't realistic, but He talked in one place about cutting off your hand if you have stolen. Or plucking out your eye if you've had lustful thoughts. Who hasn't committed those sins in their lives, at one time or another? Anybody who takes all of those verses literally needs to be committed to the psychiatric ward at the hospital!"

✦ ✦

While Sean's blunt assessment of his experience with the Bible is stronger than most, many people would have to admit that, if they are being completely honest, they, too, feel disconnected from Scripture when they try to make its contents relevant to their daily lives. Even people who discipline themselves to read the Bible regularly often find the experience frustrating when they try to harmonize the text's seemingly contrasting messages.

On the one hand, Jesus said that His Father wouldn't forgive us unless we forgive others. On the other, many verses say that all of our sins have already been forgiven. So how do we know where we really stand on that? Are we forgiven or not? How can we *know* whether or not we have sincerely forgiven everybody whom we've known to hurt us? What if we only *think* that we have, but in fact have **not**? Can we ever really be at peace about that?

One verse tells us that our sins have caused a separation between God and ourselves, while another assures us that *nothing* can separate us from the love of God. Which is it? Does the Bible contradict itself? Few

✦ ✦

believers in Christ would suggest that to be the case, but at the same time don't know what to do with these sorts of challenges from Scripture.

We could compile a long list of verses like the ones mentioned above, each of which has raised questions in the minds of Bible readers. In every quarter of the world where the Bible is read, discussion and debate abounds about how we are to understand various biblical topics. Church denominations have been formed, congregations have split, and friendships have been severed over someone's insistence about particular ways to understand biblical texts.

A Simple Answer to a Complex Question

This book will address that issue. You will find these chapters to be very easy to understand but, at the same time, you will see that they present you with a great key for understanding the Scriptures. Barriers to understanding the Bible can seem complex at times, and I'm not referring just to people who rarely read the Bible. After attending church, one comedian said, "That pastor

✦ ✦

read from the Bible with all those "thee's" and "thou's," and I didn't understand it at all. I never studied Shakespeare!"

It's understandable why those who are less familiar with the Bible stumble over some meanings that are readily accessible to other people who study Scriptures more frequently. The problem of understanding, however, is not limited to the casual student. Many people who have attended church and read the Bible for much of their lives also struggle to make sense out of its contents.

There are many good academic books that teach a person biblical hermeneutics, which is the field of knowledge that deals with the interpretation of the Bible. Biblical hermeneutics include principles that guide the serious Bible student to an intellectually honest approach to interpreting Scripture. Matters like the importance of consistency of approach, the contextual relevance of a verse, and the historical environment in which the original recipients of the text lived, are a few among the many principles included in biblical hermeneutics.

+ +

Those interpretive strategies are all helpful, but this book isn't going to address them. While an academic appraisal of this book could find it overly simplistic, I don't mind. My intent with it is not to address an academic audience. My approach to this topic is pastoral in nature. This book is written for the person who has just begun to read his Bible, or the one who is beginning to hunger to really understand it.

It is intended to offer simple help, so that the average woman sitting at home with her Bible on her lap can better make sense of what she is reading. I want the man who is committed to consistent Bible reading to avoid confusion about the meaning of verses by using the key that will be presented in this book. I want you to be able to unlock your Bible and know how to understand it and apply its Truth to your life.

The specific key discussed here can unlock the door that will open to a new and deeper understanding of your Bible. Questions about how to understand Scriptures may seem complex but one simple truth that you will learn in this book will have a profound effect on your life.

✦ ✦

What is this simple truth—this key—to which I refer? It's this:

We must read the entire Bible through a New Testament lens.

To put it simply, we need to read the Bible with "our grace eyes" instead of through the lens of Old Testament legalism. This book will explain in detail what that means and how to do it.

Our approach to the Scripture can bring us to its content with a grace perspective or a law perspective or, worse yet, a combination of the two. That's why it is so important when we read our Bibles to know that they are divided into a "New Testament" and "Old Testament" for good reason. If you want to understand your Bible, the starting place is to know what this fact—that the Bible is divided into two major sections—really means.

✦ ✦

1

Which Half Of My Bible Am I Reading?

hen you open your Bible, one of the first things you notice about the way it is laid out is that there is both an Old Testament section and a New Testament section. The choice to make that division wasn't just an editor's arbitrary decision to insert a break in the middle of the biblical story that indicated an intermission of sorts. That division between the Old and New Testaments has tremendous significance, and greatly affects how we understand the meaning of the Bible.

These two testaments show a monumental shift in how man would understand and relate to his God. We don't live under the Old Testament. We live in the "New

✝ ✝

Testament." What does this mean to us? It means *much*, as we shall see.

A person's "Last Will and Testament" refers to his or her final intentions and commitments to those s/he leaves behind when s/he dies. It is the written affirmation of what s/he intends those with whom s/he has had a relationship to know and to possess upon his or her death. It is a "Will" because it expresses the intentions of the author, and it is a "Testament" because it sets forth the evidence of his or her love towards its benefactors.

There are times in a person's life when s/he will write his or her "Last Will and Testament" more than once. When s/he does, the new one always becomes the prevailing document, and the old one becomes obsolete. There may be information in the old will that family members find interesting and even helpful in understanding their loved one's thoughts at the time, but the new will is what carries the authority regarding his or her final commitments to those that s/he loved.

The Old Testament in Scripture was a covenant that God made with the nation of Israel. It was His agreement

✦ ✦

with the Jewish nation about the relationship that He and they shared together. While there are many benefits that can be realized by those who aren't Jews (i.e. Gentiles), when we read the Old Testament Scriptures, it is important to remember that they were not addressed to us. They were given to the Jewish people.

For Whom Was The Law Given?

Speaking of these Old Testament laws, Leviticus 26:46 says, "These are the statutes, the ordinances and the laws that the Lord gave between himself and *the children of Israel* on Mt. Sinai by the hand of Moses" (emphasis added). The prophet, Moses was the Lawgiver who brought the Law down from Mt. Sinai. To whom were these laws given? To the Jewish people, "the children of Israel." They were never intended for anybody else except the Jewish people.

Psalm 147:19-20 says, "He tells these words to Jacob, His statutes and his judgments to Israel. He did not do so to any nation." Again, this passage shows that it

✦ ✦

wasn't just to *any* nation that God gave the Law. He specifically gave it to Israel, to the Jews.

What this means for us, in particular, is that the Gentiles–anyone who was not a Jew—was not given the law. We were never meant to live under the law, as these verses clearly indicate. That's not to suggest that you won't find many encouraging things there, but it is important to remember that, while the Old Testament content may at times be helpful for you, it wasn't written to you.

Furthermore, the Apostle Paul, the great apostle of grace, wrote in Romans 2:14-16: "For whenever Gentiles, who do not have the Law, do instinctively the things of the Law, these, not having the Law, are a law to themselves." Twice in one verse Paul reiterates the fact that Gentiles do not have the Law. He really makes this point perfectly clear for us.

✝ ✝

So, our first responsibility when we approach the Bible is to make this *distinction* between these two testaments, the testament of law and the testament of grace. They cannot be mixed and cannot be harmonized. As Paul said in the New Testament, "It's either law or grace, it can't be both." The difference between law and grace is indeed a great divide.

Put your finger on a random verse in the Old Testament Scriptures and you're likely to find yourself getting nervous about what you read. The reason for that is because there are many verses there in which God warned Israel about coming judgment based on her people's disobedience to Him. The testament that God had with Israel was based on mutual understanding and performance of its conditions.

✦ ✦

No sooner had Moses come down from the mountaintop at Sinai than God had him tell the people:

> "Now then, if you will indeed obey My voice and keep My covenant, then you shall be My own possession among all the peoples, for all the earth is Mine; and you shall be to Me a kingdom of priests and a holy nation." These are the words that you shall speak to the sons of Israel (Exodus 19:5-6).

Notice that the covenant God made with Israel was a two-sided covenant between Him and them. They were to do their part.

With genuine sincerity and great enthusiasm, the people of Israel replied, "All that the Lord has spoken we will do!" (See Exodus 19:8)

There is no doubt that they meant what they said, but Israel lacked a fundamental understanding about the nature of a covenant based around their keeping religious rules. They couldn't do it. No matter how sincere they were or how hard they tried, they just couldn't live up to the demands of God's Law.

✦ ✦

The Problem With Religious Rules

The Apostle Paul, a Jewish follower of Christ who would later write almost two thirds of the New Testament, had this to say to Israel about trying to build a lifestyle around religious rules:

> When we were controlled by our old nature, sinful desires were at work within us, and the law aroused these evil desires that produced a harvest of sinful deeds, resulting in death (Romans 7:5, NLT).

In other words, the law God gave them didn't do what they had hoped. Israelites thought that their problem was simply one of not knowing what to do to please God. They didn't realize that the problem ran much deeper than that. Although they didn't know that fact, their Creator had known it all along.

The problem they faced wasn't that they needed guidance. Their problem was that their lives needed to be empowered by *grace*. They needed internal transformation, not external regulations. Paul wrote that,

✦✦

...sinful desires were at work inside us and the religious rules we tried to live by actually produced a harvest of sinful actions! We were hoping to find the real meaning of life by keeping those rules but instead they only caused us to sense spiritual death!

That's what the law always has done. In another place, Paul wrote, "The power of sin *is* the Law" (1 Corinthians 15:56, NASB). Ironically, trying to live by religious rules is like trying to douse out a flame with a cup of gasoline. It has the opposite effect.

What happens, then, when a person reads the Bible solely for the purpose of finding out how to live? Her efforts backfire because the Law does what it always does by provoking sinful behavior.

Have you ever been on a diet and told yourself that you *must not* eat a particular thing? I remember dieting one time when my children, who were then teens, all worked at a pizza restaurant. I told myself, "I *cannot* eat pizza. It is way too high in calories and fat content. *I must not eat pizza!*"

✦✦

Those were the hardest weeks of my life, when it came to food. The Thou-Shalt-Not Ban on pizza that I placed on myself backfired, and it caused me to crave pizza like I'd never wanted it before! I fought it and fought it and fought it until my willpower caved in, and I went to the restaurant and told my son (who cooked the pizza), "Give me a *large* Supreme Pizza with extra cheese! And make it snappy!"

That day, I looked a lot like a recovering alcoholic who fell off the wagon and went on a binge. Except, my "thing" wasn't alcohol. It was pizza! The pizza law I had embraced led me to a hedonistic eating binge. Strict rules always do that, especially religious rules.

Israel was being taught that lesson the hard way. Throughout the history of the Old Testament Scripture, the story of their lives is one failed attempt after another of trying to keep God's Law. They couldn't successfully live by religious rules then, and you or I can't do it today, either. In fact, you were never intended to live that way.

If God knows everything, didn't He know that they wouldn't be able to live up to the Laws that He gave

✛✛

them? Yes, of course He did. Then why did He give them those Laws?

The answer has to do with the matter of self-righteousness. Although God knew they wouldn't keep the law, *they* thought they could do it. They held an exaggerated pride in their national identity. In fact, ancient Israel often reeked of arrogance over the fact that they were descendants of Abraham. So God gave them the Law to cause them to see their true condition. As we might say today, He used it to "bring them down a notch."

Pride is always a roadblock to experiencing His grace, and none is worse than religious arrogance. So the pride of Israel in the Old Testament had to be confronted by exposing the Israelites to His perfect Law, which would be like a mirror showing them their true spiritual condition.

Romans 5:20 describes it: "God's law was given so that all people could see how sinful they were. But as people sinned more and more, God's wonderful grace became more abundant" (NLT).

✦ ✦

God's answer to their self-righteousness was to allow them to see how sinful they actually were. However, being the God of love and grace that He is, when putrid sin came hemorrhaging out of their lives, He lavished His wonderful grace on them to heal and restore them so that they might see that *He* was the answer, not a system of rules-keeping.

They continually failed to live up to their part of the covenant, and became more and more contaminated by their sins. Our God, being relentlessly loving as He is, spoke to them about a day that He planned and foresaw coming. It was a day when He would be the One to change everything for them.

He described it when He said:

> Here's what I'm going to do: I'm going to take you out of these countries, gather you from all over, and bring you back to your own land. I'll pour pure water over you and scrub you clean. I'll give you a new heart, put a new spirit in you. I'll remove the stone heart from your body and replace it with a heart that's God-willed, not self-willed. I'll put my Spirit in you and make it possible for

✦ ✦

you to do what I tell you and live by my commands. You'll once again live in the land I gave your ancestors. You'll be my people! I'll be your God (Ezekiel 36:26-28 MSG).

God promised them that He would be the One to solve their problem. They didn't realize that it is only the grace of our God indwelling, empowering, and animating our thoughts and actions that can equip us to live the life we have been created to know and enjoy. We all need more than religious rules can give us. We need divine enablement that can only come from Him.

It was because He knew our need that our Father has held the winning trump card since before He had even created mankind. That winning card is the New Testament of grace. When the time was right, He set the Old Testament aside completely. In fact, it was actually declared "faulty" in comparison to the New Testament.

The Bible explains,

For if that first covenant had been faultless, there would have been no occasion sought for a second. For finding fault with them, He says:

✛ ✛

"Behold, days are coming, says the Lord, when I will effect a new covenant with the house of Israel and with the house of Judah; not like the covenant which I made with their fathers on the day when I took them by the hand to lead them out of the land of Egypt; for they did not continue in My covenant, and I did not care for them, says the Lord. For this is the covenant that I will make with the house of Israel after those days, says the Lord: I will put My laws into their minds, and I will write them on their hearts. And I will be their God, and they shall be My people" (Hebrews 8:7-10).

In the panoramic plan that He designed before the beginning of time, the God of Israel moved her closer, step by step, to the agenda that He had set in motion long before the people experienced their first failure. He would not be satisfied until humanity came to see that, when it comes to the matter of knowing Him, experiencing Him, and pleasing Him, it has nothing to do with our efforts to behave. Instead, it has everything to do with understanding that it is grace–the impartation of

✛ ✛

divine enablement–that allows us to live the life for which we were made.

To unlock your Bible so that you can understand its meaning and application to your own life, it is necessary to avoid reading the whole Bible through old covenant eyes that see rules to be obeyed. That's not what the Bible is about, and you will miss the point of Scripture altogether if you read it like an Old Covenant Jew who is still under the Law. That's not you at all! You are under a New Covenant and that fact changes everything.

✦ ✦

2

Are You Talking To Me?

The first thing to realize, then, in your coming to unlock the Bible is that the Old Testament and New Testament were addressed to two completely different groups of people. Did God inspire the Old Testament Scripture? Yes! Are we to set aside the Old Testament and have nothing to do with it? No!

While the Old Testament wasn't addressed to New Testament people, that doesn't mean there is no value in it for us. The narrative of God's working in the lives of His people still offers us much today. However, always remember this: the entire Bible is written *for* you, but not all of it is written *to* you.

✛✛

Read that sentence again, because it is very important.

The Apostle Paul clarified the matter in his letter to the Corinthians. "These things happened to them as examples for us. They were written down to warn us who live at the end of the age" (1 Corinthians 10:11, NLT). Their Old Covenant lives were an example to us in many ways, and warn us of the foolishness in thinking that we have what it takes to please God, or to live the life we were created to enjoy apart from absolute faith in Him.

I use the words, "testament" and "covenant" interchangeably, because they refer to the same thing. God's covenant with Israel, known as "the Old Testament" or "Old Covenant," called upon the people to do their part. God repeatedly told them that if they would fulfill their end of the covenant, they would be blessed, and if they didn't, they would experience all kind of curses.

What does this have to do with understanding the Bible? The answer is simple. When you read passages of Scripture that were written before the new Covenant

✦✦

began, it is important that you don't see them through the Covenant of the Law. If you read those texts with "law eyes," you will find warnings and pronouncements of judgment that will likely cause you to want to put your Bible down and not pick it up again! We must understand biblical texts through the lens of grace. It's important to remember that the verses in the Old Testament were addressed to the <u>people of that covenant,</u> and not to you.

Can you learn from their experiences? Yes! Was it written to you? No, it was not.

When we read the history of Israel in the Old Testament, we are repeatedly given the example of how trying to live independently, not trusting in God's strength and guidance, can get us into trouble fast. That is as true today as it was when Israel went her own way, instead of depending on God.

However, we must remember that we are no longer living under a covenant in which we must do our part. The idea that God does His part and we have to do our part in order to experience His blessings is one of the greatest misunderstandings that affects people today. It

✦ ✦

affects how we understand the Bible. It affects how we perceive God. It affects how we live our lives.

> Please get this point and get it well: *That is an Old Covenant mentality and you don't live under the Old Covenant!*

You have no "part" if Jesus spoke the truth when He declared from the cross, "It is finished!" He has fulfilled both His part *and* our part. Now, all that's left for us to do is celebrate with thanksgiving! In fact, that may be a pretty good definition of faith.

The New Testament of grace is completely different than the one under which Israel lived in the narrative of the Old Testament Scriptures. Do you remember the words that God spoke in Hebrews 8, quoted at the end of the last chapter? God described it in a way that leaves no room for misunderstanding. "I will effect a new covenant with the house of Israel and with the house of Judah; *Not*

✦ ✦

like the covenant which I made with their fathers" (Hebrews 8:8-9, emphasis added).

The New Covenant (Testament) is *not like* the old one. It is completely different. Not the same at all. Allow me to repeat this point once more for emphasis. How is the Old Covenant like the New Covenant? *It isn't!*

So, what will happen if we read both the Old and New Testament in the same way? We will find ourselves completely confused about what the Bible means. When we come to the New Testament, we must understand how this new covenant that God has made is different from the old one. We have to see that, not only is the old covenant outdated, it has become completely obsolete.

> When He [God] said, "A new covenant," He has made the first obsolete. But whatever is becoming obsolete and growing old is ready to disappear (Hebrews 8:13).

There is no old covenant anymore. The Old Testament Scriptures still have great value, but the old covenant is gone. It no longer exists for Israel and it never did exist for you if you're a Gentile (i.e. not a Jew).

✦✦

Mankind is now under a much superior covenant than Israel ever knew. The New Testament book of Hebrews repeatedly calls it "better." In fact, the word "better" is the most commonly used word in that New Testament book in comparing the Old and New Covenants (Testaments). How is the new covenant better? It is a covenant of grace!

What Is A Covenant?

Throughout both biblical and recent history, and still in certain parts of the world today, covenants have been very important. In the western world, by contrast, we are much more familiar with contracts. They are much more commonplace than covenants.

There are many differences between covenants and contracts, but the primary one is that a covenant carries a much, much greater level of commitment than a contract. A contract is a fifty-fifty proposition. If we enter a contract together, you do your part, I do my part, and if anyone breaks his side of the bargain, then the contract is broken, and becomes null and void. Both parties must

✦✦

keep their end of the agreement for the contract to survive.

A covenant is very different. Under covenant, two people make a bilateral agreement with a unilateral commitment. At first glance, this may sound like a contradiction but it isn't. Parties in covenant together promise one another that each one will do their part, no matter what the other person does. To enter a covenant is to say, "Even if you don't keep your part of a covenant agreement, I am going to do my part." (It is interesting to note that marriage is intended to be a covenant, not a contract. That is why we make unconditional wedding vows.)

The Old Covenant was made between God and Israel, but the New Covenant is entirely different. The Old Testament bears glaring witness that, when given the opportunity to enter a covenant with God, mankind will not and *cannot* keep our end of the agreement. We will fail every time.

For that reason, our Triune God made a *new* kind of covenant, *not like* the one He had made with Israel. This

✦ ✦

covenant would be made between the Father, Son and Holy Spirit, and mankind would have no part in keeping it. The only role humanity plays is that we are named the beneficiaries of this covenant. We are remembered in this "Will and Testament," but there are no conditions for us to keep. All we can do is receive the benefits of this Testament of Divine Love and say, "thank you!" The agreement is an internal and eternal agreement between the Father, Son and Spirit.

Are you beginning to see why this New Covenant is "better?" The benefits of this covenant don't depend on your faithfulness, but on the faithfulness of God! That, in a nutshell, is the difference between law and grace. Under law, our actions are pivotal to the success of the outcome. In grace, it all resides in God's goodness and our only role is to simply receive His blessings through faith.

When Did The New Covenant Begin?

The big snare in understanding the Bible comes when readers approach the New Testament using the lens of

✦✦

Old Testament law. Big problems arise when people don't make the distinction between these two covenants when they read their Bibles. When we don't understand that some verses are addressed to us while others aren't, the Bible becomes confusing to us.

For example, Isaiah 59:2 says, "Your iniquities have separated you from God, your sins have hidden His face from you." However, in Romans 8: 35-38, the same Bible says, "Can anything ever separate us from Christ's love?"

Does it mean he no longer loves us if we have trouble or calamity, or are persecuted, or hungry, or destitute, or in danger, or threatened with death? As the Scriptures say, "For your sake we are killed every day; we are being slaughtered like sheep." No, despite all these things, overwhelming victory is ours through Christ, who loved us. And I am convinced that *nothing can ever separate us from God's love*" (emphasis added).

Eighteenth century theologian Jonathan Edwards preached a sermon that is still heralded as a classic today entitled, "Sinners in the Hands of an Angry God." The

✦ ✦

sermon was filled with biblical warnings like this one about sin and those who commit sins: "Surely thou didst set them in slippery places; thou castedst them down into destruction: How are they brought into desolation as in a moment" (Psalm 73:18-19, KJV)!

On the other hand, Hebrews 4:15-16 says something very different.

"We do not have a high priest who cannot sympathize with our weaknesses, but one who has been tempted in every point, in all things as we are, yet without sin. Therefore, let us draw near with confidence to the throne of grace, so that we may receive mercy, and find grace to help in time of need."

The Bible plainly says in this text that, when we sin, we are to come near with *confidence* to the throne of grace. Why? Because Jesus has been through what we are going through. He didn't sin, but he knows what it is to be tempted and stands ready to offer us help.

✦ ✦

Isaiah says that your sins separated you from God. The Apostle Paul said that nothing could separate us from God's love. The psalmist said the sinner stands on the precipice of divine destruction. The writer of Hebrews says that when we sin, we should come boldly to God's throne so that we can get help. Wow! Those are two very different messages. Which one is true?

Consider another contrasting example. Jeremiah 17:9 says, "The heart is deceitful above all things, and desperately wicked." If you've attended church much, you have probably heard that verse quoted frequently. However, Paul said in Romans 6:17, "Thanks be to God that, though you were slaves to sin, *you became obedient from the heart* to that form of teaching to which you were committed." The heart, says Paul, is the motivator for obedience. Is it a deceitful and wicked heart?

Remember the verse from Ezekiel 36:26 where God promised, "I will give you *a new heart* one day and put a new spirit in you." So is it true that the heart is wicked, or do we have a new heart? Can we be obedient from the heart, or will our hearts deceive us? Which is true? Who

✝ ✝

is telling the truth? Is it Jeremiah or Paul? Or, who was right? Paul or Isaiah?

The answer is, they were both right. There is no contradiction in the Bible, just because the Old Testament says one thing and the New Testament says another. It was true *when Isaiah and Jeremiah spoke those words* to those people. However, what Paul said was true when he spoke them, too. What's the difference? The difference is the covenants under which both were speaking! Jeremiah and Isaiah spoke to Old Covenant people living in Old Covenant times. The Apostle Paul spoke to those of us living in the New Covenant.

If we fail to make the distinction between the Old and New, we will find ourselves becoming conflicted and confused when we read verses like these in the Bible. We will try to harmonize them in our minds when they cannot be harmonized. We *must* read the Bible with our grace eyes, and ask, "Is this verse written *for* me or *to* me?" The answer will make a huge difference in your understanding and your experience of the Scriptures.

✦ ✦

<u>Your</u> iniquities do *not* make a separation between you and God, because we live under a New Covenant. By seeing the New Testament through our "grace eyes," we can embrace it, accept it, and believe truth that will set us free. If, on the other hand, you don't make that distinction, you will either conclude that the Bible contradicts itself, or you'll just become a very confused person who believes that, at one moment, you can rest in God's grace, and at another, that you are in jeopardy of real trouble because you don't measure up to biblical laws. It's impossible to try to blend the old and new covenants together and come to any sense of what the Bible means. They *must* be kept separated.

Let's consider a few more examples that illustrate the point that the Old Testament Scriptures were not addressed to us, but were written under the covenant of Law, and directed toward the Jewish people. I offer these additional examples because it is so important for you to learn how to recognize what texts are to be seen in light of the Old Covenant, and which ones are to be understood based on the New.

✛ ✛

Here is one passage that I taught many times before I understood this key to interpreting Scripture. It's a verse that speaks about revival. It's a verse that has been lifted out and used to abuse many sincere people by laying guilt and demands on them.

The fact is that the word, "revival" isn't even found in the New Testament, nor is it a New Covenant concept. Like many who grew up in the church, the way I did, I often heard this verse from 2 Chronicles 7:14:

> If My people who were called by My name humble themselves and pray and see my face and turn from their wicked ways, then I will hear from heaven, will forgive their sin and will heal their land.

God is speaking here and saying, "I'm going to bless you *if* you will pray, seek my face, turn from your wicked ways, *then* I'll forgive your sin." It is a two-sided proposition, requiring fulfillment by both sides. "If you do this, then I will do that."

By contrast, Paul in the New Testament says something very different about God's grace in Romans

✦ ✦

2:4: "Do you think lightly of the riches of his kindness and tolerance and patience, not knowing that the kindness of God leads you to repentance?"

In the Old Testament, people were told, "if you repent, God will show kindness to you." Under the New Covenant, the Bible says, "God shows kindness to you and that kindness will cause you to repent. That'll make you change your mind about God, about your sin, about yourself, and many other things." Do you see the difference and the importance of recognizing both the covenant of law and the covenant of grace?

The Bible doesn't contradict itself here. It does make a distinction, in terms of the *intended recipients* of its content.

Do you understand the significance in asking, when reading any text of the Bible, "Are you talking to me?" It may be *for* you, but not be addressed *to* you. Understanding that basic principle will have immeasurable benefit in helping you apply what the Bible says in the way it is intended to be applied.

✢ ✢

3

When Was That Said?

I hope you understand now that a critical key to avoiding confusion when you read the Bible is to make the distinction between the New and Old Testaments. New Covenant Scriptures are speaking to you, but when did the New Covenant actually begin?

Many people understandably believe that the New Testament begins with Matthew chapter one. Why do they believe that? Because that is where the division is made in their Bible, between the Old Testament and New Testament. The Old Testament scriptures end with the book of Malachi, and the New Testament books begin with the Gospel of Matthew. But that division doesn't show you the important lesson you'll learn in this chapter. There's nothing wrong with the way the Bible

✦✦

editors divided the Scripture between the Old and New Covenants, but there is a truth you need to understand, or else that division can create a misunderstanding.

> The New Testament scriptures begin in the first verse of the first chapter of Matthew, but the New Covenant itself does not begin there. That may seem surprising, considering that the publisher of your Bible divided it that way.

Why would I make such a daring assertion as to suggest that the New Covenant doesn't begin in Matthew 1:1? It's because that is what the Bible plainly tells us.

Consider Hebrews 9:16-17: "For where a covenant is there must necessarily be the death of the one who made it." Jesus is the One who made the New Covenant. The text continues, "A covenant is valid *only when men are*

✝ ✝

dead, for it is never enforced while the one who made it lives."

Jesus made the New Covenant on our behalf, but it wasn't valid while He lived His human life in this world. It only became valid when He died. Hebrews 9:18 says, "Therefore even the first covenant was not inaugurated without blood." Blood always marks the inauguration of a covenant. Even the Old Covenant was inaugurated through sacrificial lambs. The New Covenant was activated upon the offering of "the Lamb of God who takes away the sin of the world" (John 1:29)!

Hebrews 10:9 says, "'Behold, I have come to do your will.' He takes away the first in order to establish the second." Jesus said to His Father, "Behold, I have come to do your will." What was the will of His Father? "He comes to take away the first in order to establish the second."

That is, He took away the first covenant. He permanently put it away, just as He permanently put away sin. Just as surely as Jesus dealt with our sin at the cross, He also put away the Old Covenant and brought

✝ ✝

the New Covenant into action. That act of grace impacts us all.

"By this will we have been sanctified through the offering of the body of Jesus Christ once for all," says the next verse.

Do you see what Jesus' offering of Himself on our behalf means for us? It means, we don't have to live by rules! It means, He has set things straight between His Father and us. He has done for us what we could never have done for ourselves. He has brought us into good standing with the Father.

To be "sanctified" is to be made holy–to be set apart by God and for God. Religious rules can't do that. They couldn't do it in the Old Covenant and they can't do it today, either, but thank God, it doesn't matter. You have been made right with God by the finished work of Jesus Christ. The New Covenant is a covenant of grace. It's all His doing, and not our own, that has positioned us in Christ.

You didn't do one thing to be in Christ. The Apostle Paul plainly said, "By *His* doing that you are in Christ

✦✦

Jesus" (1 Corinthians 1:30; emphasis added). We didn't cause it to happen because we've done something right. He's the One who did what was necessary.

Grace assures us that our place in Christ has nothing to do with our behavior. It isn't our obedience but *His* that has made us right with God. Romans 5:19 says,

> For as through the one man's disobedience [Adam] the many were made sinners, even so through the obedience of the One [Jesus] the many will be made righteous.

The Old Covenant stressed what the people had to do, but the New Covenant focuses entirely on what Christ has done on our behalf. We are challenged simply to believe it, receive it, and then live by it! His work is enough!

As a legalistic pastor who didn't understand the Bible through the grace lens for many years, I used to teach an Old Covenant, legalistic way of thinking and living. I'm almost embarrassed to admit some of the things that I used to say.

✝ ✝

"You need to get right with God!" I'd challenge my congregation.

Sometimes people would ask, "How do I do that, pastor?"

"Well," I'd admonish, "first, you need to ask God to forgive your sins. Then you need to start reading your Bible, and you need to pray, and you need to come to church, and you need to give, and you need to share your faith with others, and you need to, you need to, you need to ..."

Can't you so clearly hear the law mentality in what I was saying? I viewed the whole Bible through the lens of the Old Covenant mentality. I made no meaningful distinction between the Old and New. So I regularly chided people about "getting right with God." I thought that even those who had believed in Jesus Christ still had to do things to become "right" in the way God wanted them to be, by doing "the right things."

I wish I had understood Hebrews 10:9 then. "By this will we <u>have been</u> sanctified." Sanctified means "to be made holy, to be made right with God." How have we

✦ ✦

been sanctified? "Through the offering of the body of Jesus Christ once for all." It has already happened.

Do you need to get right with God? The Gospel clearly tells us that you have already <u>been</u> made right with God, through the offering of the body of Jesus. You are not sanctified because you read your Bible, or pray, or go to church, or give, or share your faith, or fast, or minister to the poor, or whatever your religious tradition might call on you to do. All of those things are good things, but they have nothing to do with making you right with God. You have been sanctified through the offering of the body of Jesus. It is in that way that you have been made right with God, and only in that way.

You do not need to ask God to forgive you because you have been forgiven. It's all good! God took care of the forgiveness issue in the person of Jesus. Jesus bound us all up into Himself and said, "I'll do this for you. Just as Adam ruined you, I'm going to make things right for you. Relax. You don't have to do a thing. I'll do it. Just trust Me!"

✦ ✦

"Steve," you might ask, "are you telling me that I have been made holy, and there is nothing I have to do to become what God wants me to be?"

Yes, that's exactly what I'm saying the Bible teaches. "Holy" means "to be set apart as God's possession. It means that He has separated you to Himself, for Himself." Notice that this definition has nothing to do with you and how you behave.

So, to be holy has nothing at all to do with living a squeaky clean lifestyle. The word has nothing to do with behavior. It is a word that has everything to do with *being*, and nothing to do with *doing*. It's not talking about morality. It is a word to describe your condition in Jesus Christ. It is because of what He has done, not because of what you do or don't do.

Consider these two examples. The temple in which the Jews worshipped in the Old Testament was called the "Holy Temple." A *building* was holy? How could behavior have anything to do with that? A temple couldn't behave in any way.

✦ ✦

When Moses met God at the burning bush, he was told to take off his shoes because the ground he was standing upon was *holy* ground. How could behavior have anything to do with that description of dirt? It couldn't.

"Holy" simply means being set apart. Whether you believe it or not, God has set you apart. Jesus offered his body "once for all." One act–crucifixion–for "all." That includes you.

The gospel of Jesus Christ is this good news to an unbelieving world: "God is not mad at you! He knows you and has set you apart. His finished work on the cross includes you! Whether or not you have your eyes on Him, God has His eyes on you. He has known you before you breathed your first breath." *That* is good news worth telling people!

The finished aspect of the work of Jesus Christ is real. We don't finish it by our faith. We simply experience it through believing. It is finished.

In Hebrews 10:11-14, the Bible refers to the Old Covenant period–an era described as one when "every

✦ ✦

priest that stands daily ministering and offering time after time the same sacrifice, which can never take away sins." Under the Old Covenant, priests offered sacrifices but their effectiveness only lasted temporarily. That's why they had to sacrifice offerings "time after time." The sacrifice only *covered* up the sins of the people for a year, but it could not permanently take away sins.

The verse continues by contrasting the short-term effect of Old Testament sacrifices with Jesus who,

> … having offered one sacrifice for sins for all time, SAT DOWN AT THE RIGHT HAND OF GOD, waiting from that time onward UNTIL HIS ENEMIES BE MADE A FOOTSTOOL FOR HIS FEET. For by one offering He has perfected for all time those who are sanctified (verse 14).

So it was when Jesus offered Himself that the problem of sin was permanently solved. That's when the Old Covenant ended and the New Covenant began. Anything before His crucifixion is Old Covenant.

So when you read the Bible, it is important to ask yourself, "When was that said?" If it was said before the

✦ ✦

death of Jesus, then the words were spoken during the Old Covenant and, although they can be helpful for you, they weren't addressed to you. If the words came after the cross, then you can know that, as a New Covenant child of God, the words are directed to you as a recipient of the New Covenant.

Understanding the cross as the reference point in how we interpret Scripture is central to making sure that we aren't wrongly applying verses to our individual lives that were never intended to be applied personally. This approach in no way diminishes the Bible. To the contrary, it shows great respect for the Bible and particularly for the words of Jesus, as we will see in the next chapter.

4

Aren't We To Do What Jesus Said?

"I'm a 'Red-Letter-Christian,'" Lou wrote me in an email that I received. "I believe that we are to do all that Jesus said. His words are life! We'd better take those Bible verses printed in red seriously."

While I understood his commitment to Jesus, and the desire to honor Him in how he lives his life, Lou's approach to the biblical words of Jesus was misguided. If we really want to honor Jesus, it is important to properly understand the meaning of His words, and to know what His intention was when He spoke them.

Remember that the New Covenant began specifically at the moment of Jesus' death. So, in which covenant

✦✦

period did Jesus live and carry out His ministry? I'll give you a hint that may surprise you if you've read the gospels in the New Testament. The last Old Testament prophet was John the Baptist. What may seem strange is that he isn't mentioned once until we reach the pages of New Testament Scripture, but he was an Old Covenant prophet for one simple reason. He spoke before the death of Jesus. So, if John was an Old Testament prophet because his ministry was before the death of Jesus, but he appeared in New Testament Scripture, under which covenant did Jesus live and minister?

Jesus, Himself, spoke under the covenant of law, the Old Covenant. There is no doubt that Jesus was indeed full of grace, just as the Bible says. Just watch him in the way He related to the outcasts, publicans, and sinners. Although the Law demanded death for committing adultery, Jesus didn't condemn the woman caught in the very act. Despite the fact that everybody else despised tax collectors, Jesus told Zaccheus, "Come down from that tree. I'm going home with you for dinner." He touched quarantined lepers, cried with His friends when

✛ ✛

their brother died and then raised him from the dead, healed sick people and set free those held captive by demons.

There's no missing the fact that Jesus oozed grace. He can't help it. That's just who He is. It really does look like He can't help Himself. When darkness is exposed to light, the light always rushes in to fill it. In the same way, the loving grace of the Father expressed through Jesus flooded into the valleys of broken places in people's lives.

Jesus was an Old Covenant Teacher

On the other hand, we have to understand the context of His teachings. He lived under the Law and ministered that Law to Israel, the people of the law. The Apostle Paul leaves no room for misunderstanding about this matter. He wrote, "Now I say that Jesus Christ was a minister of the circumcision for the truth of God ..." (Romans 15:8). The *Weymouth Translation* puts it: "My meaning is that Christ has become a servant to the people of Israel in vindication of God's truthfulness ..."

✝ ✝

A literal reading of the original language of Scripture describes Jesus as "a minister circumcision." The noun and adjective are reversed, the same way they are in Spanish. If you say "casa blanca" in Spanish, a literal translation would be "house white," but what you would mean is "white house." Unlike English, the adjective comes after the noun.

Young's Literal Translation says, "And I say Jesus Christ to have become a ministrant of circumcision (the Law) for the truth of God ..." Paul clearly described Jesus as a circumcision minister. Whenever the New Testament speaks of "the Circumcision," it is speaking of the nation of Israel, those under the Law. Circumcision was the Old Covenant sign of their relationship to Yahweh. So Paul is reminding us that the ministry of Jesus was to those under the covenant of the law. That means that *the teaching of Jesus was Old Covenant teaching.*

I know this concept has the potential to irritate a religious nerve, but it is an important distinction to make if you want to properly understand your Bible. Even

+ +

though He came to bring in a New Covenant, Jesus lived and taught under the Old Covenant. Get that point and it will change the way you understand the Bible for the better by not misapplying the words of Jesus.

This point is so important that I'm going to stress it once again, for emphasis–when Jesus came in to this world, He came "full of grace and truth" (see John 1:14). The Bible explains that the law was given to us through Moses, but that grace and truth came to us through Jesus. Jesus came to include us in His life and death, His burial, resurrection and ascension. What He did <u>not</u> do, however, was come to us to give us a sermon! Enjoying His life stands far above embracing His lessons. Consequently, His words in the gospels must be understood in this light.

Please don't think that I am trying to minimize the words of Jesus in any way by saying this. However, it is relevant to this point about the division between the Old and New Covenant to remember the fact that Paul describes Him as a circumcision minister. Jesus was full of grace but He lived under the law. Like other Jews, He

✚ ✚

was circumcised on the eighth day of His life, kept the Feasts, observed the Sabbath, etc. Jesus gave His life for us all, but He came to Israel.

> With that in mind, when we read the words of Jesus in the Bible, it is very important to remember the context into which He spoke. We must be mindful of *whom* He was speaking to, and *when* He was speaking.

If you are honest with yourself, you will have to admit that you have no better success applying the words of Jesus directly to your own life than you can any of the Scriptures that were written under the law. Jesus didn't come to set an example for us in how to live. He didn't come to give us teachings to guide our lives. The reason He came is to give us a "rich and satisfying life" (John 10:10, NLT). It was Life that He came to give us, and a particular kind of life.

Bios is the Greek word (the language in which the New Testament was written) that is translated as "life."

✛ ✛

However, the word refers to physical life. You'll recognize it as the root in the word, "biology"–the study of life.

What Jesus came to give us is more than bios. Although He is the source and sustainer of our physical lives, He came to give us *zoe*, another Greek word that refers to much more than physical life. The word refers to a fulfilled, meaningful, abundant, divine life. To experience *zoe* is to experience His life coursing through us!

Again, for emphasis–it wasn't a lesson but His life that Jesus came to give us. It is possible to get bogged down in His words and miss the wonder of His life! Don't miss the life of Jesus inside you by trying to create a pseudo-life built around His spoken words. He is the Living Word (expression) of God the Father.

Do you remember the verses cited by my friend Sean in the introduction to this book? He recalled Jesus speaking about cutting off your hand if you steal, or tying yourself to a millstone rather than offend a child. The reason that these words were not intended to be taken

✦ ✦

literally by us is simple: Jesus wasn't talking to us when He spoke those words.

Once again, in case you think I'm minimizing the Bible, I'm not. The Bible is true and I readily affirm that it is important to know that all of the Scripture is "given by the inspiration of God and is profitable" (2 Timothy 3:16). There may be a religious, sacred cow in your mind that causes you to flinch when I say that we can't apply everything Jesus said to our own lives. The word "repentance" involves changing our minds. Maybe this is an area of your thinking where you need to repent. It's not wrong to change your mind about this matter. To the contrary, repenting about a wrong view of anything is a good thing. We need to have a right view of the Scripture. I reiterate that the entire Bible is written *for* us, but not everything in the Bible is addressed *to* us. That includes the words spoken by Jesus.

Take, for example, what is commonly known as "The Lord's Prayer." When His disciples asked Jesus to teach them to pray, He gave an example with what might better

✦ ✦

be called "The Model Prayer." The question is, however, for whom was that prayer a model?

Jesus taught them to pray, "Forgive us our trespasses as we forgive those who trespass against us." Are we to pray for forgiveness, or do we already have it? The definitive question is, "when was that prayer taught?" Yes, Jesus said it, but to whom was He speaking?

That prayer was spoken under the Old Covenant, taught by Jesus to people who were still living under the law. That is the critical distinction of which we must remind ourselves, over and over. We do not ask Him to forgive our sins *today* because, according to Colossians 2:13-14, all of those sins have been blotted out. Paul wrote,

> "You were dead because of your sins and because your sinful nature was not yet cut away. Then God made you alive with Christ, for he forgave all our sins. He canceled the record of the charges against us and took it away by nailing it to the cross" (NLT).

✦ ✦

Paul wrote that Jesus "forgave *all* our sins." *Is that true or not?*

Is there some qualifying condition that he didn't mention? No. We can gladly know today that all our sins have been forgiven because of what Jesus did on the cross. He took the record of the charges against us, which was the demands of the Law, and He nailed it to the cross, thereby forever setting us free from its judgment. That's very different from those to whom Jesus spoke before he was crucified.

I sometimes hear sincere people say often, "If you don't forgive other people, you know what Jesus said … then God's not going to forgive you." This is just not true. Do you think that it's possible that you or anyone else will leave this world unforgiven by God because we haven't extended forgiveness to other people? If you trust in Christ but happen to die with some shred of unforgiveness in your heart, do you really think you will be locked out of heaven over that? How will you ever know peace, believing that?

+ +

If that were the case, then the work of Jesus on the cross isn't really "finished" and we can never be sure of our eternal destination until we actually reach the other side. That's a scary thought but, thank God, it is not the case. Through Jesus Christ we have been adopted as children of God. Nothing can change that.

Correctly Handling the Scripture

The words of Jesus have such importance that it behooves us to make sure that we don't misunderstand or misapply them. If you don't understand the things Jesus said in the context within which they were spoken, you will find yourself completely misunderstanding the intention of His words. We can't snatch the words of Jesus off the pages of Scripture and apply them in any way we decide. Like the rest of the Bible, the words of Jesus must be seen as He intends.

In 2 Timothy 2:15, the aging Apostle Paul wrote these words to a young pastor named Timothy.

✛ ✛

Do your best to present yourself to God as one approved, a worker who does not need to be ashamed and who correctly handles the word of truth.

For the Bible to be unlocked so that you can understand and apply its meaning to your life, it is necessary to handle it correctly.

Paul, who had been Timothy's mentor, was now coming towards the end of his life. He wanted him to get this point. It was important to him that his young pastor protégé fully understand this issue as he studied and taught the Scripture. Otherwise, not only would Timothy be confused, he would cause others to be confused, too.

"Timothy," Paul was saying, "you need to be diligent about how you handle the Scripture, the message of truth. This message in the Scripture needs to be handled accurately and presented clearly, in a way that is consistent with its true meaning."

When Paul wrote about "presenting yourself approved to God as a workman who doesn't need to be ashamed," what does he mean? He is not suggesting that

✦ ✦

God will shame you for not getting it right. Our Father would never do that. What he is saying is, "Don't embarrass yourself, Timothy. Be sure that what you're saying is in line with what the biblical text is *meaning*." There is always the potential of handling the Scripture inaccurately, and we need to strive by the power of the Holy Spirit to avoid that.

There have been times that, if I had seen from a divine perspective how I was handling the Scripture, I certainly would have been embarrassed. That was Paul's concern for Timothy. So he warned him to stay on top of the way that he studied and presented the Scriptures. He didn't want him to be one of those teachers that embarrassed himself. He wanted him to study and teach the Bible in a way that "accurately handled the word of truth."

There have been times we've all said, "But the Bible says …!" in an attempt to prove our viewpoint. Just knowing "what the Bible says" is no proof that we understand it correctly. How often have you heard

✦ ✦

someone grab random verses from the Bible and use them to support their point of view?

Almost anything can be "proven" by using the Bible incorrectly. Hitler used the Bible to justify his actions during the Holocaust. Hate groups and mass murderers often quote Scripture to support their positions. Even Satan quoted Scripture to Jesus, when He was on the mountaintop, and used the Bible to try and confuse Him. So clearly it is not enough to know merely what the Bible says. In fact, that can be dangerous. What is essential is to understand what the Bible *means*.

Are we, then, to do everything Jesus said? No, of course not. If you believe differently, I ask you why you haven't cut off your hand if you've stolen, or plucked out your eye if you've lusted. Jesus said to do those things. The fact is that you know better. You realize in that kind of extreme example that He wasn't telling you to do those things. All I'm asking you to do now is to realize the same is true of other things He said, that you have believed incorrectly should be applied to yourself.

✛✛

The words that Jesus spoke are important. In fact, they're important enough to be "accurately handled," to use the Apostle Paul's words. We honor The Living Word (Jesus) when we don't improperly try to apply His spoken words. If you believe this in some way diminishes the person of Jesus in the New Testament narrative, you will be happy to know that He Himself is the centerpiece, not only of the New Testament Scriptures, but of the entire Bible.

✝ ✝

✦ ✦

5

What Is The Topic of This Passage?

Having seen that we do a disservice to the words of Jesus when we lift them out of their context and try to apply them indiscriminately to our own lives, you may be left with a sense that the approach to the Bible that I've taught you in this book somehow marginalizes Him. Nothing could be further from the truth.

While there are just over two thousand words spoken by Jesus recorded in our Bibles, the entirety of Scripture contains almost seven hundred seventy-five thousand words, depending on which version is used. That's a small percentage of the total words in Scripture. Jesus is much bigger than the relatively few words He spoke that

+ +

are recorded in the New Testament. To build our theological views and practices around His spoken words leaves us greatly deficient in a complete understanding of both the recorded words of Jesus, and the Spirit's intention for the Scripture. There certainly must be more to Him and more to the Scriptures than the words recorded by the early evangelists inspired by the Holy Spirit to pen the biblical texts.

The wonder of Jesus stands infinitely above the things He said in the gospel accounts. Far from diminishing His biblical prominence by what I've written here about understanding His words, my goal is to help you see that He permeates the Bible. Focus on "the red letters" alone and you'll miss much of Him in the Bible. From beginning to end, it's *all* about Him!

A Christocentric Approach to the Bible

What does the main point of this book, the emphasis on reading the Bible through a New Covenant grace lens instead of an Old Covenant law lens, have to do with this chapter which looks at the place of Jesus in Scripture?

✦ ✦

Everything! While sound biblical interpretation requires that we not blend the Old and New Covenant into one, we must remember that the whole Bible is about Jesus.

Jesus Christ spans all of history as the focal point of all Reality. He was the agent in creation itself. Colossians 2:16 says, "For by Him all things were created, both in the heavens and on earth." He will be center stage at the end of all things. The last verse in the Bible says, "The grace of our Lord Jesus Christ be with you all. Amen" (Revelation 22:21).

Jesus is called in Scripture "the Alpha and Omega, the beginning and the end." That means He is the source of the start, the finish, and everything in between. That fact certainly shows itself to be true in the pages of Scripture.

There is a division in the Scriptures between the two covenants, but the one constant seamless message of the whole Bible is the grace of our Father revealed through the Son by the ministry of the Spirit. The mission of the Godhead in His relation to humanity is to cause us to see the great love that He has for every one of us. We don't

✟ ✟

have to restrict ourselves to the four gospels to see and know that love through the biblical witness. All sixty-six books set forth this great theme of the Bible.

> To accurately handle the Scripture, as discussed in the last chapter, we must come to the whole Bible with a Christocentric approach. In other words, every time we read our Bibles, we need to approach it with a mindset that looks for Christ at the center. We aren't to come to the Bible so that we can learn how to live, although that will happen. We don't read it so that we will gain knowledge of the Bible itself, although that will happen too. We don't study it so that we will be inspired and motivated by its contents, although that often will be the result. We read or study the Bible for one reason: *so that we will encounter the Living Christ.* The Bible is not an end unto itself. The Bible is the divinely inspired witness that brings us to Christ Jesus.

✦✦

Allow me to offer a personal example. As I write this chapter, I am with friends on a sailboat in the Bahamas. (There are worse places a man could work!) I love to sail. Melanie and I became certified sailors many years ago, after several trips with friends. We have sailed most years since then.

I can tell you many things about sailing. I can describe the points of sail and almost make you feel what it's like on a close haul when the wind is howling in your face, or on a beam reach when a monohull sailboat heels over with water rushing over and past the rail. I could write about raising the mainsail and the jib, about the exhilaration of tacking when the captain shouts to the crew, "Ready about?" and then, "Hard-a-lee!" I think I could describe it in a way that would make you see yourself standing on the deck as the boat moved her bow across the eye of the wind and changed course.

I could describe the relaxation of lying on the trampoline (the netting between the two hulls of a catamaran) while on a run, the wind at your back moving

✦ ✦

you gently but quickly forward. I could probably almost make you hear the sound of the wind strumming the rigging like a musical instrument, and the accompanying percussion of the sail as it luffs on a calm day when the wind is directly behind you.

In other words, I can use words to give you a good feel for what sailing on the open sea is like, but with my best and even effective description and with your imagination fully engaged, you still wouldn't get it. There's only one way to truly know the joy of sailing, and that's to sail.

In the same way, when we read the words of the Bible to learn *about* our God, there can be some benefit, but we will still miss the Real Life of the Bible. The Holy Spirit of God didn't inspire the Scriptures so that we can know about God. He wrote it to bring us into an *experiential* knowledge of God. Reading the Bible is a cognitive experience, but its purpose is to bring us to a place that transcends the mind. The Bible can touch our emotions, but its purpose is to reach deeper than that. The Bible is given to us to bring us face-to-face with our

✦✦

Creator in a way that we will stand in awe, overwhelmed and forever transformed by the present-moment, live experience of encountering His love.

There is a familiar story in Luke 24 about Jesus meeting a few of His disciples after His resurrection as they walked home down the eight mile long Emmaus Road. The men were so discouraged because they had believed that Jesus would be their king in the Kingdom of God that He repeatedly referenced in His teaching, and now, or so they believed, He was dead.

Luke describes it in verses 13-35 (*NIV*):

Now that same day two of them were going to a village called Emmaus, about seven miles from Jerusalem. [14] They were talking with each other about everything that had happened. [15] As they talked and discussed these things with each other, Jesus himself came up and walked along with them; [16] but they were kept from recognizing him.

[17] He asked them, 'What are you discussing together as you walk along?' They stood still, their faces downcast. [18] One of them, named Cleopas, asked him, "Are you the only one visiting Jerusalem who does not know the things that have

✦ ✦

happened there in these days?" [19] "What things?" he asked.

"About Jesus of Nazareth," they replied. "He was a prophet, powerful in word and deed before God and all the people. [20] The chief priests and our rulers handed him over to be sentenced to death, and they crucified him; [21] but we had hoped that he was the one who was going to redeem Israel. And what is more, it is the third day since all this took place. [22] In addition, some of our women amazed us. They went to the tomb early this morning [23] but didn't find his body. They came and told us that they had seen a vision of angels, who said he was alive. [24] Then some of our companions went to the tomb and found it just as the women had said, but they did not see Jesus."

[25] He said to them, "How foolish you are, and how slow to believe all that the prophets have spoken! [26] Did not the Messiah have to suffer these things and then enter his glory?" [27] And beginning with Moses and all the Prophets, he explained to them what was said in all the Scriptures concerning himself.

Notice in verse 27 that Jesus "explained to them what was said in all the Scriptures concerning himself." He started with the first five books of the Bible, (the ones

✢✢

written by Moses), and proceeded through the prophetic books of the Old Testament, explaining to them what the Scriptures said about Himself. They needed to see that.

Luke also describes another occasion where Jesus asserted that the Old Testament Scriptures are about Him. Luke 4:16-22 (NLT) says,

[16] When he came to the village of Nazareth, his boyhood home, he went as usual to the synagogue on the Sabbath and stood up to read the Scriptures. [17] The scroll containing the messages of Isaiah the prophet was handed to him, and he unrolled the scroll to the place where it says: [18] "The Spirit of the Lord is upon me, for he has appointed me to preach Good News to the poor. He has sent me to proclaim that captives will be released, that the blind will see, that the downtrodden will be freed from their oppressors, [19] and that the time of the Lord's favor has come."

[20] He rolled up the scroll, handed it back to the attendant, and sat down. Everyone in the synagogue stared at him intently. [21] Then he said, "This Scripture has come true today before your very eyes!" [22] All who were there spoke well of him and were amazed by the gracious words that

✝ ✝

fell from his lips. "How can this be?" they asked. "Isn't this Joseph's son?"

"This Scripture has come true today before your very eyes!" Jesus told them. He wanted them to see that He was the One Isaiah spoke of, the One upon whom the Spirit of God resided; the One who was to share the Good News; the One to proclaim freedom for captives, sight for the blind, and liberty for those downtrodden by oppressors. Those who heard Him were amazed. It was *Him!* Jesus was the One Isaiah had written about centuries earlier!

If there is still any doubt in your mind that the whole Old Testament is as much about Jesus as the New Testament is, consider the time when He was speaking to the Pharisees about their rigorous Bible study.

You study the Scriptures diligently because you think that in them you have eternal life. These are the very Scriptures that testify about me … (John 5:39).

✦ ✦

What Scriptures did the Pharisees study? They studied the books of the Old Testament. The New Testament hadn't even been written when Jesus spoke these words. Jesus told them that the Scriptures they studied were written for the very purpose of testifying of *Him*.

Remember that in each instance where Jesus told people that the Scriptures were all about Him, He was speaking of Old Testament Scriptures. There is an Old and New Covenant, and each must be understood in their proper context, but Jesus Christ stands as the Centerpiece of every age. He is the unchangeable constant who forever has and forever will reveal the love of His Father to us. To unlock your Bible, you must see Jesus on every page!

Every book of the Old Testament is about Him. In Genesis, He is the seed of the woman that would defeat Satan himself to rescue you.

In Exodus, He is the Passover Lamb who took sin's penalty upon Himself.

✝ ✝

In Leviticus, He is the scapegoat that carries sins away.

Numbers reveals Him as the guiding Cloud by Day and the Pillar of Fire by night.

In Deuteronomy, He is our Place of Refuge.

Joshua presents Jesus as the Captain of our Salvation.

In Judges, He is the One who takes weak people and makes them miraculously strong.

In Ruth, He is the Kinsman Redeemer who rescues us from disaster.

1 Samuel presents Jesus as the Prophet of the LORD.

2 Samuel shows Him to be the Faithful Friend.

In 1 Kings, He is the One about whom the half has never been told.

2 Kings reveals Him as the God who restores our cutting edge when we've lost it.

1 Chronicles assures us He is the Enlarger of our Territory.

In 2 Chronicles, He is our Shout of Victory in the fierce battles of life.

Ezra shows He is the Fulfiller of our Dreams.

✛ ✛

In Nehemiah, He is the Rebuilder of our broken walls and lives.

In Esther, He is our Protector during vulnerable times.

Job declares He is our Redeemer who in latter days will stand upon the earth.

In Psalms, He is our Good Shepherd.

In Proverbs, He is the Wisdom of God given to us.

Ecclesiastes shows Jesus to be Eternity set in our hearts.

In the Song of Solomon, He is our Lover and Bridegroom.

Isaiah reveals Him as the Suffering Servant who took sin's pain on our behalf.

In Jeremiah, He is the Righteous Branch from which our own righteousness is produced.

Lamentations brings Him to us as the One who is Great in Faithfulness.

In Ezekiel, He is the Breath that brings dry bones to life.

✢ ✢

In Daniel, Jesus is the Son of Man coming in the clouds.

Hosea presents Him as the One who forgives the worst sins imaginable.

In Joel, He is the Baptizer with the Spirit.

In Amos, He is our Burden Bearer.

Obadiah declares Him to be our Savior.

In Jonah, He is the One raised up after three days.

In Micah, He is our hope in helpless situations.

In Nahum, He is the God who turns ruin into splendor.

In Habakkuk, He is the Source and Sustainer of our faith.

Zephaniah shows Jesus to be the LORD, mighty to save.

Haggai shows He is the Cleansing Fountain.

In Zechariah, He is the Pierced Son.

And in Malachi, Jesus is the Sun of Righteousness, rising with healing in His wings.

It's all Jesus! He is the topic of the whole Bible. He is the darling of the ages and the focal point of all that

✦ ✦

exists. He is the Creator, Sustainer, and Nurturer of your life. In fact, He *is* your life. He is everything. Luke described it, saying, "In Him we live and move and exist" (Acts 17:28).

When you read your Bible, the proper objective in your reading is to encounter Him–to see and experience His presence with you and in you to show you the Father's love, empowering you to live in the awareness and power of that Love every day.

✛ ✛

✦ ✦

Conclusion

As you finish this book, I trust that you are better equipped to read your Bible so that you can understand and apply its teaching to your life in a way that is helpful. The Scripture is much like the star that shined brightly on the night that Jesus was born into this world. It is a beacon to guide us to Him.

Author Juan Carlos Ortiz raised the question in one of his books about a scenario in which the wise men might have worshipped the star of Bethlehem instead of the One to whom it led them. Can you imagine such a mistake? They would have missed the Christ-child had that happened, and yet that is exactly what sometimes happens when people come to the Bible. Because they misunderstand its content and intended purpose, they

✦ ✦

miss its Main Character. They look for life lessons, and miss the Life those lessons are intended to bring us to see and know.

If you will begin to read the Bible by asking the questions and applying the teaching of this book, you will find Jesus throughout the Bible. The Bible is like that bright star that shined on the manger. It points us to Jesus. He is in every book of the Bible.

The Scriptures have been compared to a picture album. As you saw in the last chapter, Jesus is on every page. In the pages on the New Testament, He is in the forefront of the picture and is easy to see. In the Old Testament, He often stands in the background of the texts, but is there nonetheless. To those who read these texts carefully and prayerfully, they will see Him and will be overwhelmed by His beauty and gracious love.

Many people think the Bible is a guidebook intended to give direction to us. While it certainly can do that, giving direction isn't its purpose. Others see it as a rulebook telling us what to do and not do. Nothing could be further from the truth. Still others see it as a textbook.

✦ ✦

They study it so that they can "know the Bible." But what good does that do? Simple knowledge separate from the Source of knowledge is empty, and produces nothing but pride and a false sense of security.

> If I were to call the Bible by any other descriptive name, I'd call it a gracebook. Its purpose is to show us the loving grace of our Father, as revealed to us through His Son Jesus in the power of the Holy Spirit. *That* is the heart of what authentic Christianity is all about, and what the intended purpose that the Bible is to fulfill.

✛✛

If you've read the Bible and haven't understood it, you are going to discover that the things you've learned in this book are going to help you. If you read the Bible and feel condemned, you're using the wrong lens. Throw away that Old Covenant lens and begin to read the Scriptures through the lens of the New Covenant--the one characterized by receptors that are open to the love and divine goodness which is directed toward you for no other reason than the simple fact that God *is* love.

Don't attempt to live by the Bible. That's not why God gave it to you. We are to live by the life of the Christ who indwells us. The Bible will help you understand *Him*, and what it means to trust Him to express His life through you in practical ways in your daily life.

Your Bible is the most precious physical possession that you have. Treasure it and enjoy the benefits it offers you. I've met persecuted Christians in other countries who have been imprisoned and even tortured because they owned or taught the Bible. When they were released from prison, many of them immediately returned to their practice of reading the Bible. That's how much they love

+ +

it. These devotees have seen the Holy Spirit unlock their Bibles, and show them how to understand and apply it to their lives in ways that have forever transformed them by bringing them into an awareness of their union with The Living God.

It is my prayer that the Scriptures will "come alive" to you in fresh and new ways like you've never experienced until now. I pray that you will feel your Father's love as you read, and that you'll hear His voice gently whispering words of love to you.

Don't be impatient if you don't immediately see a complete change in how you understand the Bible. Perhaps you've been reading it through a legalistic lens for a long time. Your paradigm will change. Just keep reading it through grace eyes. Discern which verses are *for* you and which are written *to* you. Look for Jesus as you read. Ask the Holy Spirit to guide you. Jesus promised that His Spirit would "guide you into all truth," and you can depend on that to happen.

✝ ✝

Finally, I would really like to hear from you if you find this eBook to be helpful to you. You can write me at **unlockyourbible@gracewalk.org.**

I also invite you to visit my website at **www.gracewalk.org.** At that site, you can find many other things to encourage you in your own grace walk, including radio programs, video teachings, articles, plus links to my other books, recorded resources, and my personal blog. I'd also appreciate your positive reviews of this book on amazon.com or wherever you may have gotten it. Positive reviews will encourage others to read it.

Thank you for taking the time to read *Unlock Your Bible*. May you be richly blessed as you revel in the grace of our Lord Jesus Christ through your study of the precious Holy Bible.

✦ ✦

About the Author

D r. **Steve McVey** is the President of Grace Walk, a ministry located in Atlanta, Georgia with satellite offices in Mexico, Canada, Pakistan, Australia, Argentina and El Salvador. For more information on Grace Walk, visit **www.gracewalk.org**. He is the author of the books *Grace Walk* (Harvest House, 1995), *Grace Rules*

✦ ✦

(Harvest House, 1998), *Grace Amazing* (Harvest House, January 2001), *A Divine Invitation* (Harvest House, July 2002), *The Godward Gaze* (Harvest House, 2003), *The Grace Walk Experience* (Harvest House Publishers, 2009), *Walking in The Will of God* (Harvest House, 2009), *Journey Into Intimacy* (Grace Walk Resources, LLC 2008), *52 Lies Heard in Church Every Sunday* (Harvest House 2011), *Helping Others Overcome Addiction* (Harvest House, 2012; co-Author Mike Quarles), and *The Grace Walk Devotional* (Harvest House, 2013). Over 550,000 copies of Steve's books have been published in fifteen languages.

Steve is the host of the daily "Grace Walk" radio program, airing across the U.S. He and his wife, Melanie, live in the Atlanta area. They have four adult children and three grandchildren.

✦ ✦

Newest Books from Steve McVey

❖ *Getting Past the Hurt When Others Have Wronged Us*

Co-written with Steve's wife Melanie McVey, this book describes how she came to find freedom and healing after suffering a horrible abuse during her childhood. Steve and Melanie have counseled hurting people for over forty years, and have seen many experience freedom as Christ led them along the pathway. In this book, you'll discover:

➢ How to recognize the effects of internalizing painful events that have happened to you.
➢ How to identify the hurts done to you that need to be resolved.
➢ How to take four biblical steps that will free you from the past.
➢ How to deal with ongoing emotions about what happened.
➢ How to relate to the person who hurt you.
➢ How to handle it when somebody continues to hurt you.

✦ ✦

Christ alone sets us free and heals our wounds. "Getting Past The Hurt" is nothing less than a description of the pathway of grace that He walks us through to experience that healing. Many have found the healing they needed, and so can you.

Available at Amazon.

❖ *When Wives Walk in Grace*

These short, easy-to-read chapters cover the most common challenges that wives face in marriage, and offer specific and practical advice on dealing with those challenges. You'll learn things like how to deal with verbal abuse, how to handle it if you feel your husband doesn't share your spiritual journey with you, how to move through arguments in a way that is helpful and not destructive, and how to balance your life when responsibilities seem to be more than you can handle. There are twenty-two chapters that deal with issues like these. You can take a look at the book or purchase it at Amazon, as well.

✦ ✦

Want To Join A Free Online Bible Study With Steve?

Every week, Steve posts a video teaching online that you can watch free at any time during the week. You can see it right on our home page at **www.gracewalk.org.**

✦ ✦

Made in the USA
Columbia, SC
04 November 2023

25476960R00059